Smile, you

SMILE!

You will live longer...

CIPRIAN OLTEANU

Smile, you will live longer...

Smile, you will live longer...

==I dedicate this book to my lovely mother Maria==

==&==

==to my beautiful wife Roxana.==

Smile, you will live longer...

Smile, you will live longer...

SMILE, YOU WILL LIVE LONGER...

Copyright © 2023 by Ciprian Olteanu

Thank you for buying an authorized edition of this book and for complying with copyright laws by not reproducing, scanning, or distributing any part of it in any form without permission.

First edition, June 2023

Title: SMILE, YOU WILL LIVE LONGER...
Text design, cover design & layout: C.O. Design Belgium

Smile, you will live longer...

CONTENTS

1. Introduction

2. Perception about smiling around the world

3. Why some people are not smiling?

4. What is smiling?

5. The 12 benefits of smiling

6. The Icebreaker and the conflict annihilator

7. Reinvent yourself and change your perception

8. What is happiness?

9. Learn how to smile

10. Smiling in photography

11. Smiling in sales and in doing business

12. Conclusion

BIBLIOGRAPHY

Smile, you will live longer...

Smile, you will live longer...

==**"Peace begins with a smile" - Mother Teresa**==

Smile, you will live longer...

Smile, you will live longer...

Chapter 1

Chapter 1

INTRODUCTION

"I was smiling yesterday,

I'm smiling today and I'm going to smile tomorrow,

simply because life is too short to cry for anything."

– Santosh Kalwar

Welcome to my story!

I am glad you chose to find out more about smiling and you have decided to discover this fascinating world of non-verbal communication!

First of all I wrote this book for you, the reader, because you see I believe that if we share our knowledge between us we can improve our lives, we can reach a higher level of satisfaction, well-being and ultimately abundance and happiness.

You know, I strongly believe our lives are a *learning process*, so as long as we are alive - we learn. That's the way it is. So the one who will tell you „I know everything!", or „I dont need to learn anymore!", or „I know enough!", – He is a fool! Right?

You never know enough or know it all. Not in this life.

There is no such think as „*I know everything*" between us, human beings.

Secondly, I wrote this book to *myself* because you see, there were a lot of moments in my life I was not happy, so I didn't really understand the meaning of being happy, nevertheless, for a long period of time I wasn't able to smile, I didn't even know how do I look when I smile... ☺

A few years ago, after I have been studying about smiling and body language, I found in an old box a photo with myself, a picture from 2002, I was smiling! and I said to myself „Wow, look at you, such a beautiful smile you have, but you never seem to use it though..."

How was that possible, so I lived all those years without even know I can smile?!

So I am still fighting with myself every single day to get these powerful tools fixed in my subconscious so that one day I can become a better person, *that* happy person.

You see, if you ask me, this is the meaning of life, or one of the most important,

To work on our personal development,

To become a better person,

To become the best version of ourselves.

In this material I have concentrated my whole experience (of about 28 years) around self-confidence and everything I have studied over the last 6 years in the field of photography, physical appearance and non-verbal communication, and I want to share all these secrets with you.

To tell you honestly, by the age of 25 I was walking with my eyes on the ground and I was practically afraid to smile, not to mention that I had great difficulties talking to someone. Now, we are all introverts and extroverts at some point, but I was the shyest person in the world.

The fact that I did *not* come from a smiling culture and in my teenager time I was not used to smile -engaged me and motivated me to delve deeper into this amazing and fascinating tool of non-verbal communication called *smile* and I decided to find out as much as possible about it.
In 2017 I began to study in detail the body language rules, gestures and posing techniques, different ways of presenting yourself in front of the camera, face and body - related.

At that time I discovered the importance of smiling in interacting with people at any social level. To dive deeper into the world of smiling, I have studied books; I have been searching for related information about well-known psychologists and body language specialists, and speakers from all over the world.

The methods you'll find in this book will help you change your vision of life, see the world differently, react differently, understand the meaning of **smiling** and its short-term and long-term benefits. This material guides you step by step towards deepening the smile as a means of non-verbal communication, helps you master the art of smiling and helps you achieve your goals through it, or at least a big part of it. ☺

This book will help you reach a high level of self-confidence, a high level of attractiveness, it will help you get what you want in any kind of situation and you will learn, literally, how to smile and how to deal with conflicts using non-verbal communication.

To tell you honestly I am the kind of person who goes straight to the point, so some ideas in certain fragments in this book are a bit exaggerated in order to make you understand my point. Also I was trying to use simple words, understandable for anybody because I strongly believe that the sophisticated words are not important in a book about personal development but what it has a huge importance are ***the idea*** and ***the message***.

Smile, you will live longer...

Smile, you will live longer...

Chapter 2

Chapter 2

PERCEPTION ABOUT SMILING AROUND THE WORLD

"Everyone smiles in the same language."- George Carlin

Sometime in the fall of 2006, after many and continuous failures in finding a job, I decided to apply for a job as a photographer (staff) on a cruise ship. What can be so complicated, I said to myself, I love to travel, there is nothing keeping me at home, I have experience in photography and what I do not know I can learn along the way (like I always did) ☺.

Said and done. I send the biography.

Along with the standard response to my request, I received the job description, more precisely the detailed daily schedule I will have to follow if I will be selected as a photographer and how I have to interact with the passengers on the ship. I was deeply surprised to see how much **smiling** matters for this function, and even more to notice that the smile actually plays the most important role for this kind of positions.

"You are part of the ship's staff, so you must have a professional appearance. Usually, you will have to wear a uniform and you must assist passengers with all their needs and requirements. Passenger safety is imperative and you will need to understand and help people as much as possible while on board the ship. At the same time, you need to manage your time and make sure you have enough time to help everyone. Being a photographer on a cruise ship can be an interesting experience, but it can also be very time consuming. Once you understand the job description of a cruise ship photographer, you will know exactly what this job expects from you.

Customer satisfaction is for us the number one priority, so your responsibility is first of all to radiate a positive energy, to be a pleasant, sociable, communicative and a **smiling person**.

-When customers go to the restaurant for breakfast, you wait in front of the restaurant, **you smile**, and you photograph each person, do not forget your gain is mostly made up of sales, so the more pleasant you are and the more you sell the higher your gain will be.

-When you get off the ship, you wait at the head of the staircase, **you smile** and you take pictures of each passenger.

-When the passengers return to the ship the same way, you take pictures and do not forget to wait for them with a **smile** on your face.

-When it's dinner time, you wait in place x, and as the passengers pass in front of you, **you smile** at them and take pictures.

After you have taken all the photos, you take care of their actual printing and interact with the passengers in Y place to sell them. Do not forget, your main priority is to sell as many photos as possible, so you must be **sociable, communicative and cheerful.**"

At the time, it seemed to me something extremely interesting, to be able to work as a photographer on a cruise ship, to be able to see the world or at least a big part of it, and at the same time to do what I love. But for understandable reasons I immediately realized that I could not work in a **daily tornado of smiles**, minute after minute, week by week, month by month.

Me?? Smiling 1500 times a day?

How can I smile all day long, if I barely manage to smile three times a year? ☺

First of all, I grew up in Eastern Europe, in Romania!

And Romania did not have a smiling culture. For us, smiling was not a priority and a way of life as in other countries, I did not see smiles in the society which I lived in and if I have seen a smile it was only in the family, or in a very small circle of closed friends. Of course I refer to the time before the revolution.

More, **I did not associate success with the way of interacting with those around me** simply because I lived in a society that didn't use the smile to interact with others; the way to communicate was (at least at that time) of a different nature.

Even though I had a sense of humor developed in general, for me success meant more to have a good education, to go to a good school, to pursue a master's degree, maybe even a PhD and to find a good and stable job and that's about it.

I certainly did not think for a moment that only if I smile in certain situations:

I might be more successful,

I could be promoted,

I could earn better at work,

I can make myself pleasant,

I can solve conflicts and

I can make new friends.

In the European countries the perception about smiling differs from one community to another, from one area to another and from one city to another, the basic idea is that already between us Europeans there are very big differences in terms of culture and non-verbal language, not to mention the differences between continents...which is huge.

Now, let's get back to the major culture differences in terms of **smiling**.

Americans are internationally recognized for their big smile, though perhaps less so in New York or other major cities. What does your smile mean in different cultures? Different cultures appreciate and interpret the smile in different ways. For example, in Russia, people do not smile because smiling (with no reason) in their perception implies that you are a man with mental problems, masked and manipulative. Even in daily family photos, people from the eastern European countries, appear with stony, serious faces.

In Japan, smiling is a way to show respect or hide what you actually feel. Although, in Japanese culture, nonverbal expressions use the eyes more than the mouth, Australians and

Canadians have smiling cultures and usually smile to show that they are happy or satisfied. Although they may not have the same reputation for huge white smiles as Americans, they smile more than our colleagues from Russia, Japan, China, Switzerland and even the UK.

So, if countries like the United States, Canada and Australia have smiling cultures and countries like China, Russia and Japan don't what does that tell us?

According to research, countries that have been built and populated with many different cultures brought together smile more often and more enthusiastically than more homogenous nations, it is not a general rule but at least in America this is how things went. When immigrants from many different cultures and languages came together and were pressured by circumstances to live and work together, they had to rely on their nonverbal communication to make connections with their neighbors.

So although Germans do not smile at foreigners, 150 years ago, when a German family migrated to the USA and shared a neighborhood with families from Mexico, Poland, Ireland, and

Italy, everyone had to learn to get along despite the differences in language. The smile played an important role in the nonverbal communication between cultures.

In order to get along with others, Americans tend to smile and reflect the favorite feelings of the people around them. As a result, they often smile brightly to show the people around them that they are happy.

It is important to remember that when considering what nonverbal behavior means in different cultures, smiling is not necessarily an indicator of happiness, at least on a large scale. For example, countries such as Switzerland, Sweden and Norway have a very high level of happiness, or rather a very high standard of living, but they are not particularly smiling cultures. On the other hand, the United States has steadily declined in the international ranking of happiness in the world happiness report, despite its smiling behavior.

In the Eastern European countries things have been a bit different, especially if we refer to Romania, we must be honest to ourselves to understand and accept the influence from the communist system and the political oscillations and the changes of situations throughout history have made their mark on the way people communicate non-verbally, the way we approach someone around us, the way we look, **how** and **when** or *if* we have to smile.

How many times has it happened to you to enter a small store and the sales person does not say a word to you? Not to mention the smile that should have appeared on the figure of the sales person *before* the greeting...
Attitude that for many years has been (in Romania for instance) perceived as something very normal.

How many times has it happened to you to notice that an unknown person fixes you? and this person looks fixed and long-lasting, not necessarily having a well-justified reason for this gesture.

Attitude matters, most of the time, more than the product. If you buy a coffee maybe not exactly extraordinary, the smile and the attitude of the seller do more than the product itself.

At the opposite pole, no matter how good the coffee is, if you meet a person with a depressive figure, it seems as if you do not feel the need to come back ever again ☺

Most of the time, such an approach translates for the client as follows: the man in front of me does not love his job, something bothers him, I bother him! The reaction of rejection at the unconscious level eases our decision not to return to the same store.

Beyond the fact that we pay time for a good or a service and we expect politeness in exchange for politeness, and as a customer, the core of our beliefs stretch to the unconscious that will make us keep away from that company for a long, long time to come, if not for the whole life.

"Almost nothing material is needed for a happy life for he who has understood existence" – Marcus Aurelius

Smile, you will live longer...

Smile, you will live longer...

Chapter 3

Chapter 3

WHY SOME PEOPLE ARE NOT SMILING?

"We have many problems in life. But my lips don't know that. They're always smiling."- Charlie Chaplin

The reasons why some people *don't* smile can be various.

==*Oral health problems*==. If you are confident with your smile, you are more likely to show it off! Better oral health is crucial to be able to smile with confidence.

==*Information technology and virtual environments*==. The smartphone era isolates you, makes you less friendly and much less prone to interacting with others in social situations. Spending the time you look at the phone reduces the amount of eye contact and smiles with others. It has been proven that smart phones distract from the present moment and can make relationships more difficult.

==*Abuse, addictions and vices*==. The use of alcohol, cigarettes or drugs can ruin lives in many ways, but it also has a significant negative impact on oral health. Even after an addiction is overcome, the damage to the teeth will remain. This can cause frustration and even setbacks in recovery. When people received dental treatment after addiction, they were much more likely to complete treatment for substance abuse and remain abstinent!

Moebius syndrome is a disorder (rare by the way), characterized by lifelong facial paralysis. People with Moebius Syndrome cannot smile or frown, and often not blink or move their eyes from side to side. In some cases, the syndrome is also associated with physical problems in other parts of the body.

The nature of the profession. Some people do not smile because their profession does not allow them. How can you expect police officers and lawyers to smile warmly at those they interact with? Models are told to keep a serious face so that viewers appreciate the ensemble they display rather than their appearance.

Society and the environment. See the differences in culture and the perception of smiling in the Eastern European countries, or other areas of the world. (Chapter 2)

Personal reasons or trauma. Some people forget to smile because of the storms of life that brought them down. The circumstances shape them into hard nuts; the experiences turn them into indifferent individuals who find it difficult to discern the light from within. The pain pushes them into darkness so they have to make a huge effort to smile.

Perception difference or being shy. Some people just aren't willing to smile. They can be shy, they may have problems of trust or they do not feel the need to smile. It can also happen that they were raised in a family or a culture where smiles were not easily offered, so if you lived in a non-smiling culture 30 years long it's difficult to understand why some people smile "just like that" and what the benefits of it are. Your perception about smiling in general it's just ***different***.

Smile, you will live longer...

Smile, you will live longer...

Chapter 4

Chapter 4

WHAT IS SMILING?

"Every smile makes you look younger every day."

Chinese proverb

The habit of smiling is present in our human being long before we are actually born!

Interesting, isn't it? Actually unborn babies can smile weeks before they leave the womb.

The smile might appear first time at 26 weeks development.

After the baby is born, he progresses to a social smile at around the age of two months. A social smile is a true smile that the baby shows in response to a parent's voice or smile. By four months of age, babies use social smiles often to engage and gain the attention of those around them, especially with the closed ones or the ones who are more often around him. It is not uncommon for a four-month-old baby to spontaneously smile at people around him for interaction.

So we can easily notice that the ability to smile exists long time **before we are born**, and definitely long time **before we start to speak**.

Later on, when we are adults we continue to use our smile to communicate, for instance we are able to recognize a smiling face from a much longer distance than a serious face (of the same person).

Let's take a look, what is the meaning of **smile** from different perspectives:

*"A **smile** is a facial expression formed primarily by flexing the muscles at the sides of the mouth. Some smiles include a contraction of the muscles at the corner of the eyes, an action known as a Duchenne smile. Among humans, a smile expresses delight, sociability, happiness, joy, or amusement. It is distinct from a similar but usually involuntary expression of anxiety known as a grimace. Although cross-cultural studies have shown that smiling is a means of communication throughout the world, there are large differences among different cultures, religions, and societies, with some using smiles to convey confusion or embarrassment."*

(Source: Wikipedia, Duchenne smile)

"SMILE meaning

: an expression on your face that makes the corners of your mouth turn up and that shows happiness, amusement, pleasure, affection, etc.

- *He greeted me with a big smile.*
- *I like your smile.*

(Source: Britannica Dictionary)

"Smiled; smiles

Smile is the thing you do with your face when you are happy — or want others to think you are. Your expression softens and your mouth turns up at the corners.

Smile, noun or verb, with its universal message and association with enjoyment and pleasure, is a very useful word. It can express joy or even say hello. Of course if you "smile through your sorrows," you are either tying to make yourself feel better or fool other people into thinking you are happy. But in general, a smile is a good sign."

(Source: Vocabulary.com)

Smile, you will live longer…

The smile is celebrated every year on the first Friday of October. It all started in 1963 when the American painter Harvey Ball was hired by an insurance company to create a smiling face that would lift the morale of the employees.

Ball created the famous Smiley face, a round yellow face with two eyes and a wide smile in just 10 minutes and was paid for his drawing with 45 dollars. Ball stated that never in the history of mankind and art has anything simpler, but understandable, been created that would bring so much joy, happiness and pleasure.

Its symbol was printed on more than half a million cufflinks and quickly became known all over the world. Smiley face has entered popular culture as a symbol of goodwill and cheerfulness, the image being used to externalize positive emotions, especially in messages transmitted by e-mail. Gradually, however, the smiling symbol was ultra commercialized and risked to lose its original meaning through its constant repetition and multiplication. From this concern came Bell's idea to establish a **World Smile Day**, so that all of us can dedicate at least one day of the year to smile and beautiful deeds, because a smiling face has nothing to do with either politics, geography or religion. In 1999 Harvey Ball decreed that the first Friday in October would become World Smile Day because it is in everyone's power to smile and do a good deed. On this day, people celebrate the smile in a creative and fun way, help those in need, organize funny events in hospitals or try to set new records of smiling faces.

Let's dive deeper into this world of smiling.

Children smile, on average, 400 times a day, while the happiest adults smile only 40-50 times a day. Consider the hidden power of the smile; it's like a superpower. But **unlike the ability to fly or become invisible, smiling can be learned, practiced and improved.**

Did you know that smiling is on the 2nd place in the top 43 habits that can make people happier?

First of all what is the definition of smiling:

==**Smiling is physiologically a facial expression formed by the inflection of 17 muscles at the extremities of the mouth but also near the eyes.**==

Before we go further we must first clarify something about the 19 types of "smiles". The 19 types of smiles that are mentioned in many articles, books, etc. are not "smiles", but they are facial expressions. Facial expressions can also express sadness, depression, fear, contempt, disinterest, so negative emotions as well. Of the 19 expressions, only 3 clearly differentiate themselves as smiles, that is, expressions collated with **well-being**, if we want to define expressions that resemble to smiley face, only one radically detaches as the authentic expression of happiness, **the Duchenne Smile**.

Let's analyze a little bit what is happening when we smile.

Smiles can mean different things, depending on the exact facial expression. There are happy smiles, shy smiles, warm smiles and ironic smiles…

While conducting research on the physiology of facial expressions in the mid-19th century, French neurologist Guillaume Duchenne identified at least two distinct types of smiles.

A Duchenne smile involves the contraction of both the large zygomatic muscle (which raises the corners of the mouth) and the orbicularis oculi muscle (which raises the cheeks and forms those small wrinkles around the eyes). Duchenne's smile was described as a "smile with the eyes".

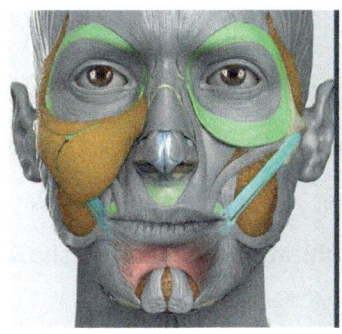

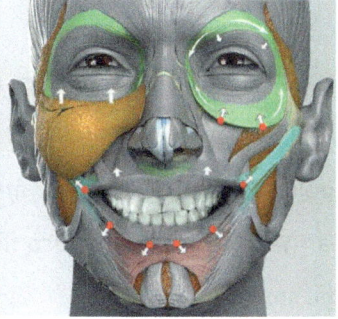

A non-Duchenne smile involves only the major zygomatic muscle. Research conducted in adults initially indicated that joy was indexed by the generic smile, any smile involving the raising of the corners of the lips. More recent research suggests that the smile in which the muscle around the eye contracts, lifting the cheeks, is associated with positive emotions.

==Smile, you will live longer...==

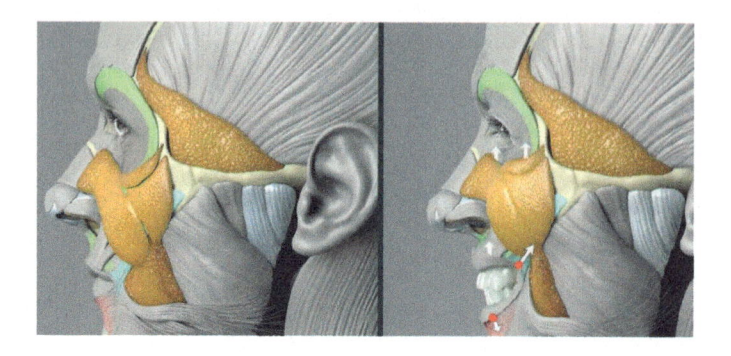

==The Smile Pan Am, is the name given to a social smile, in which only the large zygomatic muscle is voluntarily contracted to show politeness.== It is named after the current airline Pan American World Airways, whose flight attendants always show the same smile.

Why is non-verbal language so important?

Non-verbal communication is much more efficient, much easier to use and has a much stronger impact than all other types of communication.

In the graph below you can see the importance and the impact of each type of communication:

a. *Verbal communication*, is the actual expression through words to convey messages, thoughts, ideas and feelings, counts only in a proportion of 7% when interacting.

b. *Paraverbal communication*, more precisely *the way* you say something, namely the tone of your voice, the volume of your voice, the accent, the rhythm, the diction, the pauses in speech, counts in proportion of 38%.

c. *Nonverbal communication*, namely the body language, posture, gestures and facial expressions count in proportion of 55%.

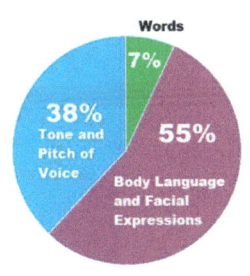

Smile, you will live longer...

Smile, you will live longer...

Chapter 5

Chapter 5

THE 12 BENEFITS OF SMILING

"I love those who smile in trouble."

— Leonardo Da Vinci

1. Smiling makes you look better

First of all, you are much more attractive when you smile! Want to be more attractive? Simple, smile! A face enhanced by a smile is definitely a beautiful face. To convince yourself of this, look at two photos of yourself, one in which you sit soberly, you do not smile, and a photo in which you smile with your entire figure. Notice the differences.

2. Smiling makes you feel better

You just feel good! When you smile, no doubt you feel better. Research shows that a smile releases serotonin, also called the "happiness hormone." Smile and you will feel happier. You are happy, you smile! Even when you're not feeling well, try to smile and see how this little trick will change your mood.

3. Have more confidence in yourself and in others

When you smile, the trust in yourself climbs exponentially and we all know that the two types of trust (self-confidence and confidence in those around you) are closely related to each other, so by smiling you increase this trusting process.

If you want to improve your credibility, simply smile more. What could be easier than that? Trust does not come easy for many, but smiling at someone will help you. It is also known that smiling increases cooperation. A smile can mean more than just a pleasant greeting.

4. The smile settles conflicts

"Beauty is power and a smile is her sword." – John Ray

A smile is an innocent gesture that expresses peace, tranquility and the desire to communicate, a gesture recognized anywhere in the world. If you find yourself in a conflicting situation, the smile gives you confidence in yourself, shows those around you that you are in control and you show that you are not afraid, on the contrary.

5. Build better and faster relationships!

Smiling is a key ingredient in establishing healthy and authentic friendships. When someone smiles at you, they show that they like you. When you like a person, what do you think at first?

I love this person.

A smile is also an encouragement to the person you are talking to. A smile is crucial when it comes to the first impression. Smiling when you meet someone, you will indicate to the other person that you are very happy to see them and that you are a positive person.

"A smile is a creator of friends." – Bangambiki Habyarimana

6. Smiling is contagious!

When the person you're talking to or those around you are smiling, you can't help but do the same. Try to smile at someone who accidentally looks at you.

7. Smiling is good for your health

You tend to think of a smile as a result of positive emotions or incentives, but it seems that your smile will be a good one. it can actually affect your stress level and productivity. The smile releases endorphins, which improves your mood, helps you relax and lowers your blood pressure. The release of endorphins through the smile also increases blood flow. The smile has been associated with an increase in HDL levels (good cholesterol) in the body and decreases stress hormones. So, smiling and laughing more can improve overall heart health!

8. Smiling improves efficiency at work

The benefits of smiling also extend to the work environment. By smiling at your coworkers, you create moments of connection that lead to greater productivity and teamwork. People who are working and interacting on daily basis with people turn out to have a more positive effect on customers when they smile. People in management positions favor their employees who smile regularly.

9. Smiling stimulates your activity

Not only can smiling make you feel happier and more positive, but it can also lead to higher productivity rates. Studies show that being happy has a significant effect on productivity at your workplace. Smiling causes feelings of satisfaction and more cheerful emotions! Satisfaction and joy lead to more productivity because you engage in a positive and happier mindset. However, the opposite is true as well: negative emotions can cause a feeling of dryness and cause us to be less productive.

10. You will be a better leader

Whether you're a leader, or you aspire to be one, smiling can be the key to your success. Smiling is an extremely effective leadership technique. It helps employees feel at ease and improves the company culture. The next time you want to show your leadership skills, smile! Impress them successfully and reach them with a smile.

11. Reducing stress and strengthening the immune system

Smiling can trick your brain into thinking you're happy, which can then stimulate real feelings of happiness. But it doesn't end there. One study shows how the mind is connected to the immune system; depression weakens the immune system, while happiness, on the other hand, has been shown to stimulate the resistance of our organism.

12. Smiling will make you live longer

Scientifically it has been proven that through laughter we live longer. It has been found that there is a correlation between depression and biological aging, so it is good to smile more and not being sad and thus to have a state of well-being and happiness. In sad people, the cells age faster. Experts have shown that patients suffering from depressive disorders can frequently develop somatic diseases that are associated with aging. They have an increased risk of suffering from cancer, diabetes, heart disease, nerve disease and obesity. That is why it is advisable to smile, this is not complicated, it helps you to look better physically and live longer.

Smile, you will live longer...

Smile, you will live longer...

Chapter 6

Chapter 6

THE ICEBREAKER AND THE CONFLICT ANNIHILATOR

"Peace begins with a smile" - Mother Teresa

I had the chance to spend a significant amount of time in the Western Europe, leaving Romania in the autumn of 2002 and traveling in the meantime to over 32 countries.

After a few years of living abroad I returned to Romania and something sensational happened to me.

Right in front of the house where I lived, a building was being made, and as I walk through the front of this yard I take a look at the yard and I see a hardworking man, sitting on some boulders, about 50 years old, who is looking straight to me.

At that moment I have tried not to fix him back so not to create a situation at least unpleasant and I took my gaze away from the person for a few moments in the hope that it would pass. After a few seconds I look back and realize that he hasn't taken his eyes off me for a moment. I look behind; maybe he's looking to someone behind me, right? It was nobody else there behind me.

I said to myself now I have to take the ace out of my sleeve. I took my heart in my teeth and smile discreetly at him. He continues to look at me with a sober figure who expresses absolutely nothing. But nothing at all.

I continue to smile at him and asked him:

-Hello, have you seen in the last 5 minutes any taxi stopping by out here? At that moment I see how his face lights up, he had become another man in a fraction of a second and he did not expect me to talk to him or to ask anything.

He answers me very serenely:

-Hello, no...Since I'm sitting here, I haven't seen a taxi stopping by...

I exchanged a few more short lines with him and I left.

In the seconds that followed I realized a lot of things, first of all this man didn't hate me, right? The fact he did not smile was not because he hated me.

He just didn't even know me, so he definitely didn't want a conflict of any kind, he was just curious to see who I was first of all, because I was new to the area (new at least for him) and he was looking at me because he usually was looking at anyone who was passing by. This was his way of seeing things. Discovering people, right?

Then it was clear that he did not know how to smile and did not use the smile as a communication tool. On top of that he was also very shy, I have noticed, so if I hadn't broken the ice he wouldn't have dared to say anything to me what so ever.

So my built-up perception in the west in the recent years about this type of person tended to be completely wrong...more precisely that, if he doesn't smile back to me he doesn't want to communicate with me.

Completely wrong!

This man doesn't hate anyone, that's just how he looks, that's how he was used to look, and YES he wants to communicate, but he doesn't dare and he doesn't know how to make it unthinkable and not be awkward either. More, he would like to smile - and maybe under certain circumstances he even expresses his happiness and he even smiles naturally, maybe with a former schoolmate or a childhood friend or someone very close to him, at home in his environment – but for an interaction with an unknown person that's his approach.

In the next chapter I will help you discover different methods of "how to smile" literally.

"Sometimes it's better to just remain silent and smile"

Smile, you will live longer...

Smile, you will live longer...

Chapter 7

Chapter 7

REINVENT YOURSELF AND CHANGE YOUR PERCEPTION

Repeat anything often enough and it will start to become YOU.
— Tom Hopkins

Your perception of life determines the reality you experience.

Whether your reality is a place of endless wonder and opportunity, or whether it's a depressing hole where all roads lead to dead ends, really depends on how you see it.

But here's the interesting thing. Reality can be whatever you make it, and you are 100% in control of that.

The key is your perception. Through your perception, you can extract so much joy from this experience. Also through your perception, you can cause yourself to suffer immensely – and make this world a place you don't want to stay in.

Perception is responsible for the quality of your life, not your material condition.

We assume that we all perceive the same reality, but everyone lives in different worlds.

==No two people think exactly alike, behave exactly alike, or have the exact same beliefs. No two people have the same upbringing, childhood, experiences, core beliefs or conditioning.==

Your life experience is molded by your perceptions of it, and everyone's perception of life is *unique*.

If you want to change your reality, you must get to the *roots*. Having a high-paying job, a nice house, a loving family is great, but you can also be miserable with all these things.

On the other hand if you have little, but you see the world with optimism, appreciate the little things, and make the most out of every opportunity presented, big or small – is this going to make you feel good about your life, or miserable?

Let's put it this way. Who do you think is happier? A monk who lives a life of absolute simplicity, or a dictator who *has it all*?

Your perception of life is responsible for how happy you are, and how much you suffer. It's responsible for how successful you become, and what you turn your life into. Your life experience is not dependent on the physical condition of it, but more on how you look at it.

Luckily, your perception of life is not fixed because naturally it's always changing. This means that your outlook on life can drastically change with a little work. It's neither a quick nor easy process, but you do have the ultimate say over how you view your experience on this planet. Will it be one of doom and despair where you need to struggle with every little thing, or will it be one of beauty and unlimited potential where the world is your friend? It depends on you.

Can you change your perception of life?

Well, actually you can!

Your perception of life refers to your general outlook of reality, yourself, and the world around you. It's thoroughly interconnected with your beliefs, thoughts, and perspectives of any situation or occurrence that happens within your life. It sets the foundation of how you will live your life, so it's important to acknowledge that.

Think of it this way, your perception of life is the result of translating all of your sensory information into something identifiable. You're always receiving information from your senses, and how you interpret this information creates belief systems.

The information you receive is objective, but your interpretation of it is not. So when you learn to interpret information in a way that benefits you, life becomes much more manageable. Everyone perceives life because we're all experiencing it. We all just perceive life in different ways, meaning that your perception of life is your individual interpretation of it.

Your course of life will be congruent with your perceptions. Therefore if you change your perceptions, you will resultantly change your life experience.

"Science teaches to think but love teaches to smile."

- Santosh Kalwar

Your perception of life is influenced by your life experiences.

How you are conditioned throughout your life molds your perception of life. This determines what you are receptive to, and how experiences are interpreted. This ranges from noticing different things, having different expectations, associations, outlooks and mindsets.

After nearly drowning while swimming at the beach, you will not see the ocean the same as you once did. Your focus will shift from an enjoyable experience to associations with fear, unease and trauma. Your negative experience conditioned you to see the beach in a certain way.

Someone who was raised in an abusive family will live in a personal reality of fear and paranoia if these traumas were not addressed. Due to their previous experiences, their reality shifts to accommodate resonating beliefs.

This person might become more receptive to other people's suffering. They are likely to notice more crime, drama, and misery in everything they experience, because they see the world as a *hostile place*.

As a result of their experiences, they live in an ugly reality.
People aren't changing the universal reality. They are *distorting* it to their own experiences.

This is usually an unconscious process. They are oblivious to it, and live in a bubble that other people do not see. In this sense, we conjure a lot of pain for ourselves in life, usually because of the way we perceive life.

Therefore it's important to address your perceptions, question why you see things as you do, and take steps to neutralize these negative perceptions.

A negative perception of life can put you into a world of pain. If you see more bad than good in everything, this is going to proliferate into negative thoughts, feelings, attitudes, behaviors, and a reduced state of well-being in general.

For the most part, **it's not your actual problems that cause suffering in your life. It's the way you view these problems.**
This means that to solve a problem, you need to get to the roots of the problem for anything to actually change.

Another fascinating concept about perception that we have to keep an eye on is the *"second arrow of suffering"*.

Basically this concept is about how you see the pain coming towards you and how you deal with it. The parable of the second arrow is a Buddhist parable about dealing with suffering *smarter*. The Buddhists say that any time we suffer misfortune, two arrows fly our way. Being struck by an arrow is painful. Being struck by a second arrow is even more painful.

From this point of view there are two kinds of sufferings.

The first kind of suffering is **unavoidable** (ex. accidents, disease, heartbreaks, old age, abuses, family problems, you name it).

The second kind of suffering is **avoidable** (this could be our perception about the first arrow, exaggerating the effect of the first arrow, refusal to accept the first arrow, and so on).

The Buddha teaches that if one is able to be mindful of the first arrow, the second arrow can be avoided. In other words, after the first unavoidable arrow is launched, the second arrow doesn't have to be launched (by ourselves).

We are able to stop ourselves from hurting ourselves further by engaging in self-destructive habits.

So what can we actually do to change our perception, where to start?

1. Smiling and laughing really are the best medicine ever

Smiling is literally a painkiller. It can kill both physical and emotional pain. Studies comparing some type of neutral distraction, relaxation and laughter found laughter to be the most effective in raising a person's pain threshold. The same is true for anger sensitivity - how touchy you are and how easily you can be provoked to anger. In other words, you're less likely to be annoyed by something if you're in good humor than if you are not.

Humor gives you an alternative reaction to choose - if you drop the birthday cake on the floor just as you go to cut it, you can throw a tantrum or laugh instead. Think of humor as a shield that protects you from the strong impact of someone else's bad behavior.

Some people seem to have been born with a great sense of humor. They don't have to try to be funny or make themselves and other people laugh – it just comes naturally. Other people have to look outside themselves to find something to make them laugh.

> "Smiling doesn't necessarily mean you're happy.
>
> Sometimes it just means you're strong."

2. Try on conscious level to bring laughter into your life:

- Avoid the serious stuff especially the news, and watch things like comedies that are light-hearted even to the point of being silly.

- Close your eyes and remember a situation where you laughed until your sides hurt. Let yourself smile.

- Find films or channels that make you laugh, and watch them repeatedly. Think of it as therapy!

- Go and buy a joke book!

- Go out to places where people are openly having fun. Carnivals, football matches, live music and events where everyone takes part - can bring instant mood improvement.

- Involve yourself in activities that provide good company. Just being with others and hearing their voices and positive vibes can lift your mood enough to make you want to join in.

- Keep photos and reminders of fun times with friends and family in your home and at work

- Spend time with people who have a good sense of humor as often as you can.

- Spend time with pets and animals. The effects can be calming as well as positive for your mood.

3. Try to hang around with optimists

A direct link exists between your attitude towards life and your mood. Generally, people are either positive or negative in their outlook:

- **Optimists** believe that things will generally turn out for the best, and tend to be in a positive mood. They see the good in people; both people they know, and people in general. Even when life seems to be conspiring against you, if you're an optimist you tend to believe in a more hopeful day somewhere in the future.

- **Pessimists** on the other hand, always expect things not to turn out well (just wait, you'll see!) and, as a result, they're more apt to find themselves anxious, worried and ready to be angry when their negative expectations are met. They're the people who, even when something goes well, they say to themselves, *"It's all going so well, something has to go wrong."* ☺

You form attitudes like optimism early in life, mostly as result of experience. They may also partly be influences from inherited personality traits, handed down from one generation to the next. Regardless of their origin, however, these attitudes remain fairly stable from cradle to grave, unless you question them, and reconsider whether they're helpful to you. Attitudes are contagious. Because they're largely learned, hanging around with people who have a positive outlook on life means that you're more likely to think and feel the same way. The reverse is true as well if you spend your time with a bunch of pessimists who see the worst in everything.

4. Be an optimist by nature. Finding the good in the bad

Psychologists have a new name for finding something good in a bad situation - it's called benefit-finding. Studies of patients with a variety of catastrophic, disabling illnesses - heart disease, breast cancer, rheumatoid arthritis, multiple sclerosis - suggest that most people can identify at least one benefit they derive from being ill. The possibilities include:

- A greater appreciation for what life offers
- A higher sense of compassion and sympathy for struggle
- An enhanced sense of spirituality, pray more
- Closer, more meaningful interpersonal relationships
- Greater introspection (examining your inner self)
- Greater willingness to openly express emotion
- Improved mood and determination
- Increased activity
- Less tension, anxiety and anger.

Now let's take a look at the positive and the negative emotions, what is what:

Positive Emotions	Negative Emotions
Amazed	Afraid
Amused	Agitated
Appreciative	Alarmed
Cheerful	Angry
Content	Anxious
Curious	Ashamed
Delighted	Bitter
Enthusiastic	Bored
Excited	Depressed
Generous	Frustrated
Grateful	Guilty
Happy	Irritated
Hopeful	Petrified
Joyful	Regretful
Kind	Resentful
Loving	Sad
Optimistic	Sorrowful
Thrilled	Worried

And think about the following:

Which one are you?

How many of these emotions are dominating your behavior?

If you would implement some of the positive emotions (or all of them, or a big part of them) in your daily life you will observe – in time – the changes and the differences in your perception about things.

5. Follow the path that makes YOU feel good.

Perception is a double-edged sword. Life isn't all drama, there's a wonderful side to it if you learn to see it. It's through life-enhancing perceptions that people build the lives they do.

From wealthy and powerful individuals to great inventors, explorers, scientists and entrepreneurs, could these figures achieve what they did without the right mindsets propelling them forward?

A musician wouldn't come to fame if he or she thought it's a waste of time. Could people construct empires if they thought they were worthless and had no ambition?

Likewise, great explorers could not have found what they did, if they didn't nurture curiosity, excitement, and crave the adventure of it.

If you have a healthy perception which encourages your development, this world becomes an *amazing* place. Through this paradigm shift, you will cherry-pick the positive elements of life, and see the best in everything.

It's important to understand that the conditions of your life don't really matter. They are simply advantages and disadvantages.

Only your mind is capable of creating and sustaining happiness, as it does with pain. Start working on changing your perception of the world to a happy medium. Focus on everything good that happens to you every day, and milk every positive experience that life hands you.

Make a habit of this and keep at it, and over time, your reality will become a VERY different place.

6. Create new pictures. We can create new mental movies whenever we choose to do so. And when we develop (and concentrate on) new images that evoke powerful feelings and sensations, we'll act in ways that support those new pictures! So, the first step is to create an image of your desired outcome. You are limited only by your imagination.

7. Picture your way to sales success. If you're involved in selling any product or service, it's vital that you see yourself succeeding on a consistent basis. If you're not getting the results you want, there's no question that you're holding onto pictures of sales mediocrity, or sales disappointment, as opposed to sales success. Right now, think about your next meeting with a prospect. In your mind, how do you *see* the encounter? Are you confident and persuasive? Are you enthusiastically explaining the benefits of what you're offering? Is the prospect receptive and interested in what you're saying? Can you vividly see a successful outcome to your meeting?

Remember that you're the producer, director, script writer, lighting coordinator, costume designer and casting director of your own mental movies. You get to choose how they turn out! By mentally rehearsing and running successful outcomes through your mind, you're paving the way for success in your sales career.

Of course, if you currently run images through your mind where the prospect rejects your ideas and has no interest in your presentation, you'll attain very limited success from your sales efforts. **You'll attract those people and those situations — that correspond to your negative images.**

Not all mental pictures can be traced to your childhood. You're constantly generating mental movies based on your relationships, career experiences and other events. No matter what the source of your mental images, you and *only you* are in control of your own movies.

Whatever the mind can think and conceive. It can achieve.

Smile, you will live longer...

Smile, you will live longer...

Chapter 8

Chapter 8

WHAT IS HAPPINESS?

For every minute you are angry you lose sixty seconds of happiness.

-*Ralph Waldo Emerson*

Have you ever been asking to yourself?

What is happiness?

How can I ever reach a high level of happiness?

What do I have to do in order to be happy?

Why do I feel sometimes that I'm lost?

Is this happiness thing an unreachable something?

Now, let's see what other sources say about happiness and about being happy:

➔ *"Happiness is a subjective emotional state characterized by positive feelings and a contented sense of well-being. It involves a sense of satisfaction, joy, pleasure, and fulfillment in life. Happiness can be experienced through various sources such as relationships, achievements, personal growth, material possessions, experiences, and quality of life. It is a vital aspect of human life and is considered a fundamental goal for most people." (Source: Chat GPT)*

→ *"Happiness is a sense of well-being, joy, or contentment. When people are successful, or safe, or lucky, they feel happiness." (Source: Google)*

→ *"Happy*
Delighted, pleased, or glad, as over a particular thing: to be happy to see a person.

Characterized by or indicative of pleasure, contentment, or joy: a happy mood; a happy frame of mind.

Willing to be helpful, as with assistance, a contribution, or participation: We'll be happy to bring a couple of salads to the party.

Favored by fortune; fortunate or lucky: a happy, fruitful land.

(used as part of an expression of good wishes on a special occasion):Happy Valentine's Day to my husband. Happy Birthday, Grandpa! (Source: Dictionary.com)"

→ *"Happiness, in the context of <u>mental</u> or <u>emotional</u> states, is positive or <u>pleasant</u> emotions ranging from <u>contentment</u> to intense <u>joy</u>. (Source: Wikipedia)"*

Further, it is been said that happiness is determined by

our genetics for 50 %,

by our environment for 10 %,

and determined by ourselves for 40 %!

What Determines Happiness?

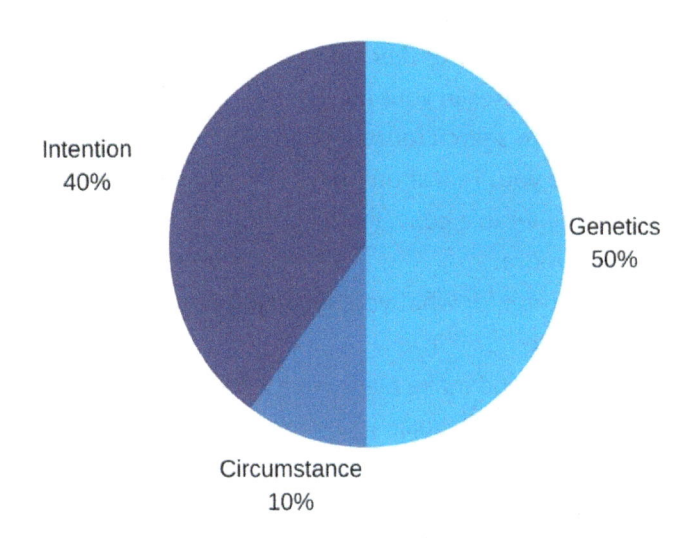

- Intention 40%
- Genetics 50%
- Circumstance 10%

Wait a second, so 40 % of my happiness levels– *that happiness* I have been dreaming of (my whole life!!!) - is determined by my own state of mind??

Hard to understand but yes my fellow friend.

Here are 28 habits you could add to your routine in order to bring more happiness in your life.

Let's strive to control our state of mind for 35% if not for 40%, so let's dive into it:

1. Accept the positives in your life.
2. Be around people who make you happy
3. Give back. Help people who might need your help.
4. Enjoy simplicity, less is more.
5. Consciously try to feel happy.
6. Find purposes in your life.
7. Value and search for real conversations with the people around you. Talk about real feelings. Engage in honest and vulnerable conversations.
8. *Smile* more.
9. Be grateful for what you have right now. Express gratitude.
10. Set goals and make plans. This will keep you motivated.
11. Happiness is a choice you make. You can choose how to be.
12. Live a healthy lifestyle. Exercise. Eat and sleep well.
13. What you *think* is becoming your reality
14. *Believe* in God and in yourself.
15. Practice positive affirmations to yourself and to others.
16. Don't be afraid to experience new things.
17. Don't look for perfection. If you always keep asking for something else in your life you don't have time to enjoy what you already have. Embrace *imperfections*. Accept and cherish the things as they are.

18. Use your time wisely. At the end, the time is the most *precious* thing we have.
19. Spend less and more efficient. Don't spend too much money on yourself – without reason.
20. Don't miss the meaningful moments along the way. *Slow down* and enjoy the little things in life.
21. Engage and hold on to your passions.
22. Evaluate your mood as often as possible.
23. Give unconditional.
24. Solve problems one at the time. Avoid multitasking.
25. Learn to say no.
26. Touch and embrace.
27. Learn to say *please* and *thank you*. These two key elements will boost your confidence and at the same time you will become more likeable.
28. Stop comparing yourself to others. It will not change anything anyway. You are **unique**.

==*The richness is giving happiness to other people - Napoleon Hill*==

Some more facts about happiness:

1. How does technology affect our happiness?

Does having more Facebook friends make you happier?

A recent study shows widespread social media use leads to reduced day-to-day happiness. Researchers mention that the Happiness and Friendship Paradox is a critical factor for reduced happiness. This is when people appear and feel less popular than their friends on social media. Negative feelings may be induced based on the feeling of lacking a robust social network.

Studies have shown that frequent digital media users also report lower psychological well-being than those who use it less. Researchers suggest these findings may be misleading since most studies do not account for other outside influences that may impact well-being, such as trauma and genetics. They claim other mechanisms, such as displacement of more beneficial activities for well-being, such as face-to-face social interaction and upward social comparison, are to blame for low well-being. These findings suggest one does not need to be a social butterfly to be happy, but it may help to have a few close friends.

2. What constitutes happiness in the workplace?

Workplace studies have shown a relationship between happiness and success in the workplace. Happy employees are likely to have a higher annual salary than unhappy workers.

Researchers found that happiness correlates with workplace success. Happiness precedes this success, and cultivating positive feelings improves the workplace. Focusing on being more satisfied at work may lead to more success in the workplace.

3. What is the optimal income for happiness?

Does more money mean more happiness? The results vary! Economists have found joy determines economic outcomes since it increases productivity, impacts labor market performance, and predicts one's future earnings.

Social research suggests that relative and absolute income significantly and positively correlated with happiness. Relative income is one's income weighed against the current standards of the day and in relation to the population's income. In contrast, absolute income is simply the total amount of income received. Higher-income at both levels is associated with higher levels of happiness!

Another study proposed a theory with the takeaway that it depends on how people conceptualize happiness regarding monetary success. Those who view happiness as having material and economic success will be happier than those who do not.

Researchers in applied economics analyzed 100,000 people from representative samples in 82 countries. They found that **personal income significantly positively impacts emotional well-being.**

When people acquire more income, their emotional well-being increases quickly and drastically.

So here's the bottom line:

Emotional well-being strongly correlates with income.

Source: Resolution of the Happiness–Income Paradox (Scienceofpeople.com)

4. Which are the happiest countries? (the first places)

Finland

Denmark

Iceland

Switzerland

The Netherlands

Luxembourg

Sweden

Norway

Israel

New Zealand

Austria

Australia

Ireland

Canada

Germany

United States

United Kingdom

So why are the Nordic countries the happiest? Regarding citizens subjective well-being, economic factors like GDP don't matter as much as social ones do! This is likely due to The Nordic Model: Standards set and followed by Norway, Sweden, Iceland, Denmark, and Sweden characterized by high living standards and low-income disparity merging free-market capitalism with a generous welfare system. The citizens of these countries all highly rate key factors for happiness:

- **Social support**
- **Freedom**
- **Generosity**
- **Trust in institutions**

(Source: World Happiness Report)

Happiness tends to exist under four main conditions:

- **Feeling content or satisfied.**
- **Being an agent of one's happiness.**
- **Emphasizing inner enrichment over material satisfaction.**
- **Maintaining a positive outlook on the future.**

Empirical researchers define happiness as the combination of life satisfaction plus subjective well-being.

Multiple factors can contribute to one's happiness:

- **Genetics**
- **Education**
- **Personality**
- **Marital status**
- **Financial situation**
- **Number of friends**
- **Amount of time spent on activities**
- **Stress and ill health**

(Source: Annual Review of Public Health: Happiness and Health)

5. Why was happiness different 200 years ago?

Researchers examined people's happiness over time by investigating cultural and historical variations in concepts of happiness. They analyzed the definition of happiness in Webster dictionaries from 30 countries over 200+ years.

For a long time, happiness has centered on circumstances outside one's control, such as fortune and good luck. During the rise of western American society, the definition of happiness has shifted towards something that can be controlled and actively pursued.

6. Are women or men happier?

Wondering how gender can affect happiness? Are women or men happier? Research shows when it comes to gender and sex, the results on who is happiest are mixed.

Data from 160 countries showed that women worldwide report higher levels of life satisfaction than men yet report higher levels of daily stress.

A 2015 Gallup World Poll examined the life circumstances and individual happiness levels of men and women in 73 countries.

In nearly all the countries, there was no significant difference between men's and women's happiness scores.

When factoring men and women with the same life circumstances, women were happier in nearly a quarter of the countries. Researchers wondered if this could be due to country characteristics like economic development, religion, or women's rights. They did not find evidence suggesting an association between the female-male happiness gap and country characteristics.

In the United States, researchers investigated men's and women's subjective health and happiness and how factors like socio-economic status impact the sexes. They found that men's health and happiness are strongly shaped by **employment**, while women's are more significantly shaped by **educational and marital status**.

7. Why does having friends increase happiness?

The Harvard Study of Adult Development is one of the world's longest studies of adult life, collecting data on people's mental and physical health since 1938, aiming to uncover the factors leading to healthy and happy lives. Researchers found a strong association between happiness and having close relationships with friends and family.

When it comes to health and happiness, it is well-established that:

- Happiness buffers stress by preserving health and encouraging longer life.

- Happiness positively affects life satisfaction by increasing mental well-being.

- Health and happiness are positively correlated at all ecological and social system levels, such as individual, regional, and national.

"Silence and Smile are two powerful tools. Smile is the way to solve many problems and Silence is the way to avoid many problems"

Smile, you will live longer...

Smile, you will live longer...

Chapter 9

Chapter 9

LEARN HOW TO SMILE

Whether you think you can - or think you can't - you're right!
Henry Ford

If you can turn your smile into a habit, then you can turn *happiness* into a habit!

Before applying the methods of smiling naturally, start with the relaxation phase of the facial muscles. Relax your eyebrows and jaw muscles.

If you feel tense, your smile will seem a little forced and you could create additional wrinkles around your eyes and eyebrows. Take a deep breath and relax the muscles of your face before you start smiling. Try to open your mouth and close it several times, try to do the same with your eyes, close them and open them several times. Relax your facial muscles.

1. **Begin by *practicing the social smile* (the smile of the stewardesses).**

Start by practicing your professional smile (or Pan Am smile). It may seem ridiculous, but most people can't tell the difference between fake and real smiles in an ongoing interaction.

Please don't get me wrong, I don't want to encourage you to practice a shallow smile or to smile only halfway just for the sake of getting over anything easier, or hoping that in this way you will conquer the world and remain in this concept, I would simply like to emphasize that by practicing the mimicked smile, the movement of the facial muscles, practicing daily or as often as possible, to slowly reach the authentic smile, the natural smile, perceived by those around you as the real smile, full of real emotions.

It has been found that the act of smiling - even if it is false - fools the part of the brain associated with happiness and the release of endorphins. The brain cannot tell the difference between the physical act of the fake smile or the real smile - for your brain, it is the same thing. So when you start practicing the fake smile, your brain thinks you're happy, and if you do it often enough, it will eventually create an authentic, happy and natural smile.

2. **Visualization and imagination method**

Think of something funny. Try to remember a funny story, a good comedy, a good joke or think about puppies or elephants that stumble, you can easily find them on Instagram ☺. Any funny memory, no matter how trivial it may seem, will make you think of a smile, a moment of relaxation and tranquility.

3. **Mirror method**

Practice your smile in the mirror, when you're alone.

Stand in front of the mirror and look at yourself as you smile. Remember that you will try to smile more often today and you will have to continue practicing.

If you want to learn how to smile, go to the mirror in the bathroom or bedroom and smile. You can do this a few times a day and adjust it until you're happy with your smile.

Analyze each phrase individually. Eventually you can take a picture and compare your smiles.

You can analyze step by step the *ideal* opening of the mouth, the distance between the lips and the *ideal* opening of your eyes – the distance between the eyelids. You will notice that some situations benefit you and others do not.

Cover your mouth with your hand and focus on the top of your face, more precisely on the nose, eyes, eyebrows and forehead, the place where wrinkles appear when you smile naturally.

4. **Selfie method**

Calm your mind and reduce your stress before you smile for a photo. Smiling to order, such as for a photo, can be stressful! The stress of achieving a perfect smile can cause the facial muscles to tense, which leads to a false or even scared look. To manage the stress caused by the smile, take a moment to close your eyes, relax the muscles and take a deep breath.

This is sometimes called the "face of social media". You don't have to make duck lips ☺ - instead, smile naturally, and then try different smiles before taking a picture of yourself.

Think of it as if you were grounding yourself and centering for a great performance, as a singer, an actor or an athlete would do.

Photograph several poses and analyze yourself. Notice the difference between smiles and expressions and give yourself time to choose the ideal smile or the smile that benefits you the most.

5. The method of interaction with others

It could be your friends, family members, pets, or your favorite book. When you are happy or satisfied with the things in your life, you are more likely to smile more often throughout the day. You can look to spend time with positive, cheerful people, full of life; you can also focus on situations and activities around you that make you happy.

After you test all this above mentioned ways analyze the result and fine tune where needed.

"Learn to smile at every situation.

See it as an opportunity to prove your strength and ability."

— Joe Brown

Smile, you will live longer...

Smile, you will live longer...

Chapter 10

Chapter 10

SMILING IN PHOTOGRAPHY

"Smiles are always in fashion!"

Old photos are a window to the past. From looking at old photos and how people looked back then, you can start to imagine what their lives were like. But have you ever noticed that most old photos feature people in formal wear looking annoyed or sometimes even downright miserable?

There is a reason why people didn't smile in old photos. In this chapter, we'll delve into the history to find out why people in the past seemed lost of happiness, even in their wedding photos.

Why people didn't smile in early photographs?

The first photographs were taken in the 1820s, with developments coming throughout the rest of the century. However, in the days of early photography, people smiling when their photos were taken was practically unheard of. So why didn't people smile in old photos?

While there's no definite explanation on why people rarely smiled in old photographs, there have been several theories posited by history experts. Here are five likely causes why people **didn't smile** in old photographs.

1. BAD TEETH & ORAL HYGIENE

Since professional dentistry was still in its infancy during the late 19th century, it stands to reason that people back then didn't have the best dental health and were likely missing teeth. This could mean that bad teeth were a common condition, and opening your mouth in social situations was something rare. However, this common explanation is relatively weak since a person can smile without having to show their bad teeth.

2. EXTREMELY LONG EXPOSURE TIMES

Back then, taking pictures with cameras used to take forever due to the long exposure time. Getting your photograph taken would be like sitting for a painting, but worse. Subjects had to sit down for up to several hours and maintain the same expression the entire time; otherwise, the image would come out blurry. Understandably, a flat expression is much easier to maintain than a happy face.

However, advancements in camera technology call this theory into question. By the 1850s, portrait cameras would have a considerably shorter exposure time. Cameras at the time would take up to one minute to take pictures, a marked improvement over early cameras.

3. PHOTOGRAPHY WAS A "ONCE IN A LIFETIME THING"

Nowadays, we can snap pictures anytime we want with smart phones. But back then, photo-taking was still very new and for the average person, a once-in-a-lifetime thing. Some people even take photographs of their deceased family members in a trend called post-mortem photography.

Since it was seen as a passage to immortality and a record of how they looked in life for future generations, most people put on their "best faces" in vintage portraits. Smiles were seen as a temporary thing, and even professional humorist Mark Twain was dead-serious in his vintage portraits. In one of his books, Mark Twain even said that he didn't want to go down in history forever with a foolish smile fixed forever on his face. So you notice that perception about smiles at that time was quite different comparing to now.

4. INFLUENCE FROM OTHER ARTS

Old paintings greatly influenced the early days of photography, because both arts "immortalize" people as they were at the time. Most people even thought the two were basically the same art form – which is understandable because they had to sit still for hours all the same.

Similar to painted portraits, people see photographs as the most important document of their life. This means they had to put on their most serious faces to make sure they were remembered as great people by their descendants.

5. CULTURAL FACTORS

The last possible explanation is likely the most plausible one – and the simplest. Long ago, people simply looked down on smiles. In Victorian and Edwardian times, silly smiles were closely associated with madness, drunkenness, and lewdness.

Since people didn't want to be seen as a drunkard or a madman with a goofy grin for the rest of time, almost every single person decided to put on a serious face when it's time to get their portraits taken.

This explanation becomes even more plausible when you take people from other cultures and social standings into account. Take this photo of an African-American man from 1860 and this photo of a Chinese man from 1904 who smiled broadly, for instance.

It's very likely that only people from Europe held the tradition of not smiling in photographs. Furthermore, they may be directed by their photographers to look as elegant as possible for the most important document in their lives.

When Did People Start To Smile In Photos?

After a century of people putting on the most serious faces for a photograph, you might be wondering when exactly did people started to smile in images. How did the norm shift from dour faces to wide smiles and naturally happy faces?

The answer is mainstream accessibility.

George Eastman introduced the Kodak camera in 1888. This camera was considerably less complicated than any that came before it and was also bundled with an instruction manual.

Eastman later doubled down on bringing photography to the general public with the Brownie camera in 1900. Geared for children and sold at an affordable $1, everyone could take black-and-white photographs easily.

By placing cameras in the hands of amateurs and the mainstream public, Eastman started a seismic shift in how people took photos. With his camera's extremely short exposure times and never-before-seen accessibility, photography was fundamentally changed.

Before, getting your photograph taken was the moment. Families would dress up in their best clothes and put on their most serious faces so their descendants would remember them as great people. After the advent of mainstream cameras, you took photos to record a moment – capturing the little things that happen in life for you and your family to look back on in the future.

Kodak's advertising further implanted the idea of smiling in photos into the public consciousness. Their catchphrase of "you press the button, we do the rest" and ad campaigns featuring smiling people urged people to start smiling in their photos as well. The ads enforced the idea that smiling in a photograph was desirable, and people just started doing so after seeing Kodak's advertisements without asking why.

As the norms of amateur photography were cemented by Kodak, the notion of smiling in photographs started bleeding into formal photography. The art of portrait painting would start to take notes from its sister art form as well, resulting in people starting to smile in portraits painted in the late Edwardian years. In other words, *smiling in photos became contagious.*

The popularity of motion pictures in the 1920s was also influential to the notion of smiling. By seeing the full range of human emotions represented on screen, it became popular to document all human emotions, not just the most dignified ones.

After several decades of this shift, smiling in photographs became the norm by the time World War II rolled around.

How to have an amazing smile when posing in photos? Smiling might be the norm in photography nowadays, but nobody said it would be easy. Sometimes, our attempts at smiling for the camera might end up silly, awkward, or just *not right.*

Despite being a natural thing for humans, smiling for cameras is something that you have to practice. So here are my seven tips plan to make sure you put on the best and the shiniest smile today!

1. RELAX YOUR FACE AND JAW MUSCLES

Nothing ruins a smile like nerves. Your nervousness tends to show clearly on your face, making your picture look very awkward. A good tip to fix this is to consciously relax your face and jaw muscles. After a second or two of doing so, your smile will look more natural for the picture.

2. THINK HAPPY THOUGHTS

The logic behind this tip is as simple as it gets. Happy thoughts make you happy. And when you're happy, you smile. As you're posing for the photograph, think about things that make you happy. Whether it's your partner, puppies, or ice cream, hold that thought in your mind. These happy thoughts tend to manifest as natural smiles in photos.

3. DON'T SAY "CHEESE", TRY ANOTHER WORD, like for instance "MONEY" or "HONEY" ☺

Despite being the go-to word for smiling when getting your picture taken, "cheese" doesn't really get the best smiles. The long "e" sound tends to make smiles look too wide and unnatural.

As an alternative, you can say the word "money". Your lip movements will make a more natural smile when your picture is taken. Plus, the thought of money can also be a happy thought for some, putting even better smiles on their face ☺

4. LOOK AWAY BEFORE THE SHOT AND TAKE A DEEP BREATH

Smiling for the camera is one thing, holding it as the photographer prepares the shot is another. Sometimes your smile will start out nicely, but become more strained as the seconds pass – just like people in old times when they had to hold the same expression for minutes. So how do you get a photo taken without staring at the camera for an uncomfortable time?

It's simple: just look away. When the photographer is preparing his shot, look at the ground or somewhere else. Then, when the photographer begins his countdown, look at the camera and smile like you just ran into your friend on the street. This way, your smile is fresh and natural because you don't have to hold it for more than a couple of seconds.

5. MAKE A JOKE OR THINK AT ONE

Few things cut through tension like a joke – good or bad. If you're finding it hard to hold a happy face, ask your photographer to tell a joke just before snapping the photo. If it's a good joke, then they'll capture a genuine laugh from you. If it's a bad joke, there's bound to be a good laugh as well. Either way, the photographer's going to capture a genuine expression!

After you test all this above mentioned ways analyze the result and fine tune where needed.

6. LOOK AT SOMEONE YOU LOVE OR SOMEONE YOU TRUST (when the photograph is being taken)

When you look at someone you love or someone you trust, an old friend, or your love partner, the pupils are getting bigger, and the light in your eyes is changing, therefore your face changes at that moment. So at this point you will look better, relaxed and more confident.

7. THINK POSITIVE

Think at yourself in a positive way, you are beautiful, you are smart, you are great, you are thankful, you feel good. All the positive feelings and sensations create a positive moment.

Remember to go back to chapter 8 - LEARN HOW TO SMILE.

Smile, you will live longer...

Smile, you will live longer...

Chapter 11

Chapter 11

SMILING IN SALES AND IN DOING BUSINESS

"Nothing you wear is more important than your smile."

– Connie Stevens

The smile triggers positive emotions, including optimism and confidence. And optimistic, confident salespeople win more and bigger sales.

A smile is one of the most basic and universal indicators of openness, friendliness, relaxation, and likeability.

Improve your business! Business can be done simply by smiling. One of the first things sellers learn quickly is to smile. Who do you prefer to buy something from? From a sales representative who seems bored, angry, frustrated or from the one who is smiling and looks happy?

A person who smiles is excited about the product he presents and will convey a positive feeling to the buyer. Even those who sell over the phone are encouraged to smile when they talk, which is felt in the way they talk.

Remember that good customer service is an essential condition for a good product or service; in fact, a 2011 study showed that 86% of customers left a company due to poor customer service.

- A good smile can increase self-confidence by up to 10%, studies have shown. This impression can be seen by people as a vital component in the sales process.

- It helps create a good first impression about your business; a customer will always prefer to do business with someone who looks or seems to be happy.

- Smiling improves your mood and therefore the attitude you face with everyday situations, including sales work and customer support.

- A smile is contagious, and people tend to copy your emotions, so a good attitude on your part can also improve the attitude of your customers; this will help you a lot in the sales and assistance process, even if you are in an interview for negotiating your salary.

Smiling happy faces are fairly common in the marketing context, like an unspoken consensus among marketers. Of course, it seems like the most obvious thing to do; you want the person associated with your product to at least look like they're enjoying it, right?

But, is there more to it? What is the science behind the smile? Or, is it as simple as the audience responding to it subconsciously in the hopes of becoming more like the person in the picture?

> *"Smile! It increases your face value."* – Robert Harling

Why Does The Smile Sell?

The appeal of a smile works, because of a phenomenon known as <u>emotional contagion</u>. In healthy bodied people, our mirror neurons work when we're exposed to a recognizable facial expression. If that facial expression is happy, our mirror neurons make us brighten up automatically.

It works, because we simply feel better when we see other people happy.

That's how we're wired.

Therefore, a smile on a models face has the ability to ignite consumer joy and improve our attitude.

A smile is a powerful and incredibly simple tool to include in your advertising arsenal. With a proven track record, a smiling face has the ability to enhance consumer joy and increase brand appeal.

Every emotion we see is contagious (thanks to mirror neurons) so make sure that when experimenting with emotional advertising, you do so cautiously.

Work on advertising your brand's "true" smile. A Duchenne smile has proven to be more effective. Use models who are smiling with their whole face and that are experiencing the emotions you are trying to convey; otherwise the smile may have an undesired effect.

People buy from people.

More importantly people they trust, and people they like.

A genuine smile doesn't just make us feel better. It makes other people feel better about us... and makes them smile too, especially during tough times.

- **SMILES IN SALES SEND A MESSAGE**

A beaming smile tells someone that you're glad to see them. That you're confident about yourself and your job, you love what you do. That you believe in what you do and the product or service you sell. A neutral face or indifference, on the other hand, is much more *ambiguous* – and makes it more difficult to close a deal.

- **SMILES (IN SALES) ARE CONTAGIOUS**

Louis Armstrong, Dean Martin, Ella Fitzgerald, Judy Garland, and Frank Sinatra are among those who sang, *"When you're smiling (the whole world smiles with you)."* And there's some truth behind those lyrics. Not only do smiles spark a feeling of reward in others, but we also have an instinct for facial mimicry – meaning people quite literally smile with us if the smile's a genuine one. So the simple act of smiling isn't just a show of *confidence or happiness, or both*. It's a mood-booster to those around you, and an important part of building trust.

- **SMILES IN SALES GO BEYOND FACE-TO-FACE**

You don't need to meet someone in-person or face-to-face for a smile to transmit warmth. Smile on a phone call, and most people on the other end can tell when you're wearing a

Duchenne smile (these auditory smiles could be just as contagious as visible ones, too).

And don't forget to smile when you're writing. Your positivity is an emotional contagion that transmits even over social networks. Your negativity does too, for that matter. So mind your mood when you write.

- **SMILES IN SALES HELP US EMPATHIZE**

The smile on your face – Duchenne or otherwise – is a window into your inner state. Mimicking someone else's smile can help you distinguish if it's a true smile or a sarcastic one; a strained one or an embarrassed one. The same goes for other facial expressions, too – trying them on yourself can help you feel what others are feeling.

In fact, when asked to empathize emotionally with others, we often do this kind of mirroring without realizing it!

- **SHARE YOUR SMILES WITH OTHERS**

We get it, there won't be a reason to smile every day, especially in this climate. Think of a smile in these situations as you would social distancing, sometimes it's for the benefit of others around you.

A smile alone doesn't guarantee sales success. It takes more than two muscles to pull that off. Still, top performers tend to share some common traits, including empathy and emotional awareness, which are closely tied to a cheerful disposition. And in a race to be more buyer-centric, it's an important tool in your toolkit.

So, put a smile on your face and make the world a better place.

The 7 body language pillars in your non-verbal communication that will make you a top seller:

- → Don't protect your chest with your hands or other objects
- → Open your palms while you speak, our hands show to the world we communicate with that we are vulnerable (Ex. I have nothing to hide in my hands), show your hands, be open, and be vulnerable
- → Shoulders back and down
- → Move slowly
- → Turn your head slowly
- → Walk with confidence, purpose and control
- → *Smile more and smile with your eyes* (Duchenne smile)

==And the top 12 characteristics you *need* to become a top seller:==

1. Independence
2. Good looks, well-dressed
3. Positivity
4. *Communication skills/Body language (verbal/non-verbal)*
5. Sociability
6. Intelligence
7. Passion
8. Sense of humor
9. Ambition
10. Confidence
11. Being proactive
12. Being likeable

==*"Beauty is power; a smile is its sword." – John Ray*==

Smile, you will live longer...

Smile, you will live longer...

Chapter 12

Chapter 12

CONCLUSION

"Everywhere you go, take a smile with you." —Sasha Azevedo

First of all we have to be aware that the perception about smiling around the globe can be *different* from a community to another, from one city to another, from a country to another.

Secondly, you have to analyze the world around you and see how the world you live in, how people see things and how far you want to go with understanding and using your non-verbal communication. Look around you, at your workplace; in your neighborhood; in your family and see if you can practice these non-verbal techniques and the effect they have on short on long-term on the people around you.

There are things in life that cannot be learned, and there are things in life that **CAN** be learned, *smile* is one of them.

You can change your perception about smiling and about being happy even if you are born and raised in a non-smiling culture, and even if according to your genetics your don't have the most happy roots in the world.

Let's be clear, you cannot do this overnight, so don't think that in two days you will be the greatest non-verbal communicator ever and the greatest smiling guru, but with discipline, a lot of practice and good will, you will eventually be able to see the things differently and take action.

In fact, if you practice a lot and if you discover what works best for you, you will be able to communicate ONLY through smiles if you decide to do so – however this will work only with certain people, who are using the same behavior frequency like you.

As you can notice smiling is strictly related to happiness although we have seen the list of the happiest countries around the world (these are not specifically the biggest smiling cultures), on the other hand you can meet people who are used to smile quite often and the country they live in is not particularly a happy one…

Today to be honest, after I have discovered these amazing effects of this smiling behavior I use my smile every single day in my daily non-verbal communication.

I like to communicate (sometimes only through smiles) with people or with kids in the supermarket, or just on the street, of course I observe immediately if the people around are willing to join the game or not and if it's not the case I just stick around to see if there are other ice breakers available in order to create a connection.

I am so happy when I pull out a smile from a non-smiling person or from a "not smiling every day kid" or "I have not been smiling for a long time "someone.

And yes, believe or not **the income is related to our happiness level** (see the statistics), although there still are a lot of communities around the world **with low income and still living a very happy life**. (Think about Africa or Thailand).

Why do you think these people keep on smiling?

Because *smiling* is the most powerful and important asset they have...

Because they use that every single day and it's something coming from the bottom of their hearts, and if this is coming from the bottom of your heart you can get what you want, sooner or later...Right? You will show your emotion and your vulnerability.

So if there is something amazing I have learned in Thailand it's that even if you posses nothing material, but nothing at all, you still have your **smile** and you could eventually be happy.

And nobody can take your beautiful smile away...

These are the moments that give you a peaceful feeling of satisfaction, a fascinating sensation that confirms you are not alone on this planet; even if we speak different languages, we stick together, I am on your side and you're on my side...We share the same planet...Right? ☺

You see, when we smile, we are sending to the others different vibrations and different messages, some of them very complex and profound, and this is equal to a storytelling if you want, like for instance:

"Hey, I like you" (Smiling),

"Hey, I accept you",

"You are welcome in my neighborhood",

"Welcome to my store" (Smiling),

"It's nice to have you around"...

"I'm open to communicate with you",

"Don't be afraid, it's ok to be shy"…"I was shy as well once, I know what you feel, and I understand you, I'm on your side"…

"Look at my hands, they are open, I have nothing to hide, this is me, and you can trust me" (Smiling)

"It's OK, I am good person…tell me, what do you want to know about me?"

"See you next time…Take care!" (Smiling)

We exchange our smiles and our happiness, at least for a moment…

Smile, you will live longer...

=="A smiling face is a beautiful face.==

==A smiling heart is a happy heart."== — *Dr. T.P. Chia*

Smile, you will live longer...

Smile, you will live longer...

BIBLIOGRAPHY

Smile, you will live longer...

BIBLIOGRAPHY

- MANAGING CULTURAL DIFFERENCES, Robert T. Moran
- BODY LANGUAGE, Joe Navarro
- UNLOCK POTENTIAL, Ken Cooper
- HOW TO UNLEASH THE POWER OF YOUR MIND AND MANIFEST SUCCESS, Clary Collins
- BODY LANGUAGE FOR MANAGERS, Horst Ruckle
- NO EXCUSES! THE POWER OF SELF-DISCIPLINE, Brian Tracy
- THE SELL, Fredrik Eklund
- PICTURE PERFECT POSING, Roberto Valenzuela
- THE STORY OF GUILLAUME DUCHENNE DE BOULOGNE, Wikipedia
- CHANGE YOUR PARADIGM, CHANGE YOUR LIFE, Bob Proctor
- ATTITUDE IS EVERYTHING, Jeff Keller
- ANATOMY OF FACIAL EXPRESSION, Uldis Zarins
- ANGER MANAGEMENT FOR DUMMIES, Gill Bloxham, Doyle Gentry
- THE PSYCHOLOGY OF SELLING, Brian Tracy

Smile, you will live longer...

Smile, you will live longer...

==*"Remember to smile"*- Nelson Mandela==

Made in the USA
Monee, IL
24 August 2023